1x 7/12 LT 6/09
1X 8/16 LT 6/09

Moving Out And Moving On

Guide for Female Teens and Their Mothers

Brenda Hayes

Moving Out And Moving On

Guide for Female Teens and Their Mothers

Brenda Hayes

MILLIGAN BOOKS   BOOKS   CALIFORNIA

Published & Distributed by:
Milligan Books, Inc.
1425 W. Manchester Avenue, Suite C
Los Angeles, CA 90047
WWW.Milligan Books. Com

Cover Design
JJ's Word Processing Services
ladyjjubilee@yahoo.com

Typeset/Format
Joe Ann Johnson

First Printing June 2005
1089765432

ISBN: 0-976768-7-2

Acknowledgments

This is a book dedicated to my daughter, Courtney. I have had many blessings in my life, but she has been the greatest! Everyday I thank God for giving me such a beautiful, loving and caring daughter.

I hope this book will not only help my daughter, but other daughters and other mothers whose daughters are about to branch out on their own!

I was raised with a mother who loved me; however, she never really expressed her feelings or knowledge about life! I remember her Sex Talk was, "Never let a boy make a fool of you?" (So what did that mean)? When it was time to take the course on Menstrual Cycle, my cousin had to convince my mom to let me take the course. My mom feared they were really going to teach me about having sex.

Can you believe that my mom threatened me? She said that if I ever moved from home without being married, that I could never come back home (of course this put the fear of God in me); and needless to say, I lived at home until age 27!

I want this book to guide my daughter and other young ladies about some of life's lessons, hoping to help prepare them for the real world ahead of them.

To my beloved daughter and every young lady, the sky is the limit - Fly Baby Fly!

About The Author

Brenda Hayes was born in Los Angeles, California. Her parents, James & Velma Cooper (both deceased) migrated from the state of Mississippi to follow their dreams to find a better life.

Brenda's parents taught her and her siblings, Linda & Donald, that a hard days work has never hurt anyone and believe me; they lived this through example.

Brenda has been married to her supportive husband, Edard (known as Ed) for 20 years. They have one child, Courtney, who is the inspiration for this book, Moving Out And Moving On.

In Brenda's spare time, you can find her reading novels, attending church or going to the newest plays in town. One of her greatest pastimes is creating new games to be played at family functions.

Brenda's future goal is to explore new adventures and challenges, along with furthering her education. Just maybe, she'll follow Courtney to her college.

Brenda's prayer is that our youth be safe, happy and successful...

Foreword

Books are written for many reasons, but this publication, **Moving Out And Moving On**, is a unique and unselfish compilation of some of life's experiences. Readers searching for information on teenage roles, expectations, and pitfalls in an ever-changing society, will find them here.

The author, Brenda Hayes, has written this book for her daughter, Courtney, as well as for the benefit of all who read it.

Featured are easy to understand guidelines to help female teens through adolescent years and into young adulthood. No stones are left unturned as the author has painstakingly included hotline information that covers a wide range of topics from dating, domestic violence, and sexually transmitted diseases. She has also included helpful hints that provide remedies and simple solutions.

The material is presented with an unusual flair and style. At times, readers may find themselves laughing or even crying because what she writes hits home or opens up sensitive areas.

My experiences interacting with young people as an educator for over thirty-five years prompts me to write this foreword. It is my belief that readers who are searching for frank and honest answers to what others may view as simple and trivial, will find them in this book.

Congratulations Brenda, on your insightful work, and may it be a blessing to all who select it for their reading pleasure and enhancement.

Margaret Crump Johnson

Moving Out and Moving On is a life jacket for female teens and their mothers. Consider it a life-support system available to you now. Let's face it—most parents learn through trial and error, which leaves them often feeling inadequate and guilty when some of those same errors are played out in the lives of their children.

It is *time out* for the "via trial-and-error-cycle." Let's teach our children the lessons we've learned, so they don't have to do it—the hard way. Being transparent is not a bad thing, if it drives home the lessons needed for your child to make better choices in life. Our children need to know what the behavior is that we want them to mimic and the behavior they should avoid. Nothing is off-limits!

The author is in-your-face with the truth and the facts of life. She does not skirt around life issues. She cuts to the chase. She is like an *up-to-date* and *out-of-the-box* grandmother, who imparts life's "Gems" and "Pearls of Wisdom" as you sit at her feet and listen. It is purely conversational. Hayes tells you simple truths, like getting pregnant is **not** an accident. An accident is when you cut your finger while cooking. Accidents occur when cars run into each other. An accident is when you slip and fall.

She even leaves a message for the time of earthly transition. This is a no-holds-barred book.

This book is humorous, educational and thought provoking. It's a must-read for every teen and every parent or caretaker of teens. It's an unassuming blueprint for the development of wise and healthy teens.

Dr. Rosie Milligan, Counselor

TABLE OF CONTENTS

Preface

Moving Out, and Moving On, is a book geared towards female teens, adults and their mothers. However, there are readings for everyone's appreciation.

For the mother/father who is scared to talk about it, for the single dad who is too shy to mention it, for the young teen too nervous to ask, and for the grandparents who would never think it!

This is a comical and touching account of what our young ladies will encounter in their growing years. This handbook is as real as it gets!

I originally started this book on life's lesson for my own daughter who was preparing to leave for college, however, I knew in my heart that not only my daughter, but daughters of tomorrow and years to come would benefit from the content of this book. Every school, church and youth center should have this book in their library.

I am so excited about this book and I truly believe it will catch the attention of all readers (young & old). Without a doubt, every reader will find themselves, a friend or family member inside this book.

When a daughter or loved one packs their bags to leave home, make sure they pack this book on top.

Introduction

When my 17-year-old daughter was preparing to leave for college, I thought, *Is she ready?* I wondered if I had sufficiently prepared her for the real world. I wondered a thousand *what-ifs*. I often questioned if she would be able to bounce back from mistakes when she made them.

My daughter has her stubborn side; yet, I hoped she would not be so hardheaded that she wouldn't listen to some of what I have tried to teach her. I, too, realized that at some point, I had to let go—I had to lean on my faith, prayers, and God to take care of her and guide her.

My daughter never envisioned that I was a teenager at one time; that I had partied with the best. Her mind was blown away when she saw my old photo album with pictures of guys that weren't her dad. She couldn't believe that once I had it going on (ha-ha!).

She often told me that I needed a life (smile). Well, baby-girl didn't realize that I have a life, and that she has been the greatest part of it! She didn't realize that I took motherhood as seriously as the breath I breathe.

I decided to write my daughter about some of life's lessons. I wanted her to have a part of me to take with her when she went off to college. I hoped my words would be a source of strength for not only her, but also for other young ladies out on their own for the very first time.

May God bless and direct you all!

Chapter One
The Dating Game

Straight from home with that lost look. All you need is your camera hanging around your neck (ha-ha). Believe me, you will stick out like a sore thumb.

Baby girl, this will be the test of all times. The guys will look at you like "fresh meat"! They are probably rubbing their hands together and giving each other high fives. They are sizing you up and ready to play you like a deck of cards.

Honey, be strong! Don't listen to the slick lines of, "Baby I'm here for you;" "I'll be your momma and your daddy." Girl, he will tell you how you'll never be lonely as long as he's around. Well believe me, he has just told this same line to five other girls. Don't be naive and anxious; good things can come to those who wait.

Don't make a reputation for yourself. Remember, you have your whole life ahead of you. You can't quit every job or school because you're ashamed of your actions. And don't have to walk around with your head hung low.

Keep in mind, there are double standards for a man who sleeps around, compared to a woman who sleeps around.

That man is considered a stud, the cats meow, the Mac Daddy. She is the slut, the easy piece, and the horny desperate chick!

Be selective with the choices you make in life. Slow your roll.

Girl, he is all that and a bag of chips! He is the perfect everything. I never have to want for anything. And good looking; honey, he is my Mr. Goodbar (ha-ha). And let me tell you - he has a touch that would put out a forest fire (Smoky The Bear would be jealous).

Girl, hush your mouth! You need to stop talking and bragging too much about this guy. The only person you need to tell how good your guy is - is your guy!

Don't tempt others to want to test the waters. Don't make them want to see what is so good about this guy. They may not necessarily want him, but they may just want to mess up your good thing. They may just want the pleasure of shutting you up.

And when your guy is visiting, don't always have your friends hanging around your place (like they are paying rent).

I'm a young man just trying to make it, but no one will give me a chance. I have two kids I need to take care of.

I've tried to get a job, but they only want to pay me minimum wages, and I can't deal with that. Plus they wanted me to start at 6:00 a.m. (Hey, I'm not a morning person) and since my license is suspended, I would have to get up by 4:30 to catch the bus.

Honey, if you meet this type of guy, put on some Nikes and run (don't even look back). And please don't think you can change this guy. Believe me, if his mother, ex-girlfriends and his kids couldn't motivate him to change, what makes you think you can? Heck, he can't even change for himself. And ladies, please stop making excuses for this guy. We all make choices in life, and we all have to be responsible for our choices. We can only blame others for so long for our lack of succeeding in life.

Every relationship won't always be equal in life, but make sure the other person is bringing something to the table (and not just to the bed).

Don't ever get hooked up on just a physical relationship.

I have a problem with this, and you should too! Some of these slick, smooth talking guys will try and fill your head with this garbage. Trying to make you feel that you need them; and that you should even be glad they are with you.

Honey, their goal is to demean you and lower your self-esteem. They want to keep you dependent on them.

Ask yourself, "If I am as bad as he says, then why is he with me?" Girl, wake up and smell the coffee. Believe me; just like he wanted you, someone else will want you too.

This joker is trying to keep you scared! He has you too scared to even leave his behind. He has you believing that you will be alone forever if you leave him, so you stay and continue to take his physical and mental abuse.

It's time to stop the abuse.

Young ladies, please don't fall for this one. A guy will sometimes try and make you feel guilty; guilty about what you should and could be doing for him.

Let me tell you! Don't even get tricked into believing that love equals stupidity. Love yourself first. Don't ever give in to that head game that guys can play on you when they want sex, money or special favors.

Some slick guys will try and make you believe if you loved them, that you would be willing to do anything to make them happy.

Girl, keep in mind, self preservation. Be true to yourself, and never love any man more than you love yourself.

The Big Step

No sex, until you are mentally and physically ready. Don't be persuaded or forced into things you know you don't want to do. And make sure you don't date out of your league (because some guys can really be freaky).

You may run into guys who are asking for group sex, rough sex, video sex, etc., etc. Some guys will try and run a head game - saying, "If you love me, you would want to please me in every way." He will even try and convince you that oral sex is not sex, but it is. You have to remember, this guy will tell you anything to get his rocks off; because it's all about him.

Oh, and honey, what about the slick one? The one who says, "If you don't do it, I'll find someone who will!" Believe me this is just a ploy. This type of guy is probably already slinging his Johnson everywhere. Don't be just another notch on his belt.

Learn to turn the tables on him! Tell him if he loved you, then he wouldn't try and force you into doing things you are not ready for.

Ladies, please, please don't rush into having sex, thinking this will keep your man, because it won't.

When you think you are ready for the big step, please use protection. Some guys will come up with all types of excuses for not wanting to use a condom. Like the guy who told his girlfriend that he was allergic to latex. Well, you better tell him that you are allergic to herpes, gonorrhea and dying.

Don't ever let anyone abuse your body. Make sure you always take care of your goodies.

Mom, I'm pregnant, but it was an accident!

Honey, an accident is when you cut your finger while cooking. Accidents are when cars run into each other. An accident is when you slip and fall.

Please explain to me how a penis accidentally slips into a vagina? This was not an accident; this was a direct and intentional hit. What happened to the protection you and he should have been using?

Please don't tell me he promised to get up in time. If this guy can't get up in time to go to work, or get up in time to go to school, what makes you think he can get up in time, when he's enjoying what he's doing? Believe me, it's not as easy as you both think. It would be interesting to know how many kids were born because of the "get up theory".

If you are having unprotected sex, you are setting yourself up - not just to become pregnant, but also to encounter sexual diseases. If you don't want a child, you better protect yourself. If you don't want to encounter catching sexual diseases, you better protect yourself. Don't ever put your life in someone else's hands.

Don't get tricked by a guy begging you to have his child, because you may just end up raising this child by yourself. He is now the Lone Ranger! The only time you see him is when you're in court trying to get child support.

Ladies keep in mind; single women are more accepting of a single man with kids, than a single man is of her kids. Most women will think of his kids as little darlings; however, most men will consider her kids as baggage.

If you do become pregnant, realize that you're not the first and you definitely won't be the last. It may get rough at times, but you can make it. Surround yourself with supportive people, and network with other mothers who can teach and guide you.

Play with fire and you'll be burned. If you can't stand the heat, stay out of the kitchen.

Ladies, ladies, ladies, it only takes a few seconds for guys to rise to the occasion. Be careful what you start, because he is hoping that you're going to finish it!

Girls, stop the teasing. Don't get too hot and heavy with this guy and then all of a sudden you say, "Oh, I can't." You got this guy all heated up. Honey he is about to burst; and all of a sudden you say, "Oh, I don't like you that way!" He is probably thinking, what is wrong with this nut?

If you feel weak, but not ready for sex, play it safe and go out in groups. It's okay to just hold hands. It's okay to kiss and say good night. But girls, when you get to lip locking too hard and groping one another, look out! Oh, and that tongue in the ear will get you every time (smile).

Don't start any, there won't be any!

Bad Boys

Girl, what is the attraction for these bad boys? What do they have going on so good, that girls love so much?

How many times have I heard, I don't like so and so because he looks like a nerd? He is boring, and he doesn't know how to dress. Honey, you better rethink some things. That bad boy may be the sharp dresser, knowing all the latest dance moves and can talk rings around a circle, but you better watch out!

Bad Boys are trouble walking. They have more game than the NBA. You can't win with a bad boy. Think about it! You say you want someone who is going to treat you like the queen that you are. Well honey, you are wishing on a star. Do you really think he is planning on treating you like a queen, when he knows he's the King?

Most bad boys don't have enough time or money to put you on a pedestal because he has too many other honeys lined up.

Let's look at the big picture. You can either date the not so popular guy who has goals and drive, or you can date the guy whose biggest goal in life is to get the hottest new shoes in style and some new studs for his ears.

Incognito (aka) Mystery Man

You meet this great looking guy with a smile that makes you fall to your knees. He has the charm of a saint!

The kicker is, you have been dating for months and you only have his cell number. No home or work number, and definitely no address. Duhhhhhhhh, what are you thinking?

Believe me this man is living a lie. Either he is married, has a live-in girlfriend or he is on the run (ha-ha). By the way, check his left hand for a ring tan (he may just keep removing his wedding ring when he comes around you).

Honey, what happened the other night? You spent money getting your hair done nicely. You found the cutest little outfit and you smelled oh so nice (new perfume). Well, you sat there for an hour waiting on him. He didn't show - nor did he call. Unless he was dead or in a comma, there is no excuse for this disrespect.

Again, keep in mind, people will treat you the way you allow them to. Set the tone early on in life.

Be determined that you won't allow people to disrespect you.

Who Am I Without A Man?

You are a woman, a life and a child of God. Never, ever feel that you are nothing without a man. Learn to like you. Life is so good and full of adventures.

Take time to find you. Take time to bond with family and friends. Tell yourself that you are a beautiful creation of God and that you are a blessed person.

Often times, ladies break up with one guy and run right into another relationship because they can't stand being alone.

Stop and slow down. Take time to heal and re-examine some things. And ladies, stop settling for less.

Stop accepting anything, just to say you have a man.

Mom, I thought things were going good and all of a sudden he started acting strange. He stopped calling like he used to, and when I call him, he has attitude.

Well baby, Valentine's Day is next week. Let me tell you something! If a guy is cheap, broke or scared of commitment, he may just disappear around Christmas, Valentines Day, or your birthday.

However, check yourself also. Have you been hinting around for gifts that you know he can't afford? This guy may just feel that there is no way he can afford to buy you what you've been hinting around for. He may just feel that there is no pleasing you!

Stop reminding him of how Bill is buying Tiara a gold bracelet (like you always wanted); and why can't he buy you one? If your boyfriend is working a part-time minimum wage job, you know his funds are limited.

Momma's Boy

Oh, you got your hands full. Some of our men are still boys, because their moms won't let them grow up. Some moms are forever making excuses for their sons who are lazy and have no idea how to handle their own business.

If you ever decided to marry this type of guy, you will be expected to take on where mom left off. A momma's boy will literally drain you! Can you imagine being a mother to him and to your kids at the same time?

They always say, if you find a man that is good to his mother, he will be good to you. Well, there is a big difference from being good to your momma, and being a momma's boy.

If you are the type that wants to be needed, then this may be the type of guy you want. But, on the other hand, if you want an independent, self sufficient man, then assess the situation before you jump and say yes.

Caution! Caution! Caution! If you decide to date a guy with kids, be prepared for possible drama. Again, if you knew from the start that he had a child, then don't expect smooth sailing all the time.

Never ever mistreat a child! Normally, it's not the kid causing the drama, but the woman or man behind the child. If you have a child and you are always causing the drama, that new guy in your life may just get the hell out of Dodge.

It is what it is! Either you can learn to adjust to his kids (and their momma) or you can't.

If you do decide to date a guy with kids, make sure some rules (yes rules) are established.

Treat their child how you would want yours treated.

Night Rider

This is a guy who only comes over late at night. For some strange reason, he is too busy to come over when restaurants and theaters are open (wonder why)?

To be frank, honey, he is only coming for a "Booty Call". He has no plans on taking you out and showing you a nice time. Either this guy is broke, cheap or just doesn't want to spend time treating you the way you deserve to be treated.

Again, not only men, but also people in general will treat you the way you allow them to treat you. Baby girl, you deserve more than just being some man's toy at night. Life is about giving and sharing. It's about being fair to one another.

How will you two ever grow and learn as a couple if the extent of your relationship is restricted to the bedroom? And, does he always come empty handed? It would be nice to see him walk in with some dinner, movies or some flowers.

Believe me, he may not be taking you out and spending money on you, but he is spending it on someone! Listen to his conversation. One day he will slip and say how good the play was, and you'll think, what play? We didn't go to any play!

Wake up, ladies!

Honey, he will tell you; don't play crazy because you knew how I was from the start!

You meet this person, and you think they will eventually change. You have concluded that you will work your love magic on him and he will buckle under the pressure. Girl, I am here to tell you that what you see is what you get.

People are who they are. Don't ever think you can change a person to be what you want them to be. If you don't like a loud obnoxious person, then don't get involved with them. If you don't like a person who is a drinker and party animal, then walk on.

If you met that man in a club, you can bet he is not going to stop clubbing just because you asked him to.

I'm not saying that people can't change, because they can, but only if they want to. However, if they are happy being the way they are, why would they want to change?

Also, keep in mind, if they make the sacrifice and change for you, there will be a price to pay. Be ready to hear, "I changed for you, now what are you going to do for me?"

My Name Is Not Bitch

I may be moody, and even mean at times. I may seem stressed and depressed, but my name is not Bitch!

Most men will never understand a woman because he doesn't have the nature of a woman!

How would they be if they had a monthly period, and two breasts swinging in the front of their chest (ha-ha, if you got it like that); not to mention those cramps, yeast infections, bad hair days and just every day life problems?

When their mothers, sisters, and aunts whom they love dearly, are going through the same mood swings, do they call them Bitch? I doubt that they do. I'm sure they chalk it up to they are having a bad day, or they are tired.

So that same respect they have for them, they should have for us!

Don't be anyone's Bitch!

Ladies, we have to set the tone on how we are to be treated. Stop doing too much too fast for guys.

A lot of guys are accustomed to getting and having everything done for them by ladies. We have created these problems. Guys are used to being spoiled and not being made to be responsible dates or husbands.

Some guys will take and take from you, then move on to the next lady expecting the same. They will have the nerve to tell you how well they were treated by their ex, and they expect the same from you.

It's time for ladies to let men be men! Stop doing everything for them.

Babe, don't always be the squeeze on the side; be the main dish! Be the one meeting the family, the one being introduced as his girlfriend, and the one being taken out and shown the nice time.

I bet if you show this page (or dating section) to your boyfriend, he will bash it. However, I bet these are some of the same things he would teach to his own daughter or sister.

Honey, he doesn't want his game messed up, however, he surely doesn't want this same game played on those he loves.

Don't be surprised if your book disappears; he may have just given it to his sister.

Just because this one guy was all that and a bag of chips, doesn't mean he is the only one who is. Don't rush into things and scare the poor guy away.

We as women sometimes rush into thinking, "Oh he is the one!" You have concluded that you, he and Junior (baby named after him) will live together as one big happy family. Baby girl, this guy will run faster than the wind can blow if you start this happy family talk. Remember, most women are more emotional, while most guys are visual.

Take your time and build a friendship. It's okay to just be friends. Having someone to go out to dinner, to the movies and even to church wouldn't be a bad idea either.

Most guys think of sex as just that - sex! Don't assume he is in love with you and wants to build a relationship because you two had sex.

Don't set yourself up for hurt! Slow your roll.

Oh no, kick him to the curb. There is no excuse for you to stay with a man who is hitting you. Some of these guys will hit you and then turn around and say, "You made me hit you."

Women have been beaten because they failed to answer the phone on the second ring, or because dinner was not ready on time. And don't you dare get home late, because you may get a slap upside the head for that, too.

Ladies, please don't buy into this! We are responsible for our own actions. And believe me, if he hit you once, 99.9% of the time he will hit you again. Please don't have any kids by this man or you will never get rid of him.

Ladies keep in mind - don't let your mouth write a check that your behind can't cash! In other words, don't provoke any of these men either. This doesn't make it right, but don't aggravate any of these hot-tempered guys. Please don't put them to the test.

Proverbs 22:24 says, Do not make friends with a hot-tempered man. Do not associate with one easily angered.

In the prime of her life, it was cut short. She was dating a young man she said was a charmer. Well, this charming young man decided if he couldn't have her, then no one could.

Ladies, please don't lead people on. Don't mess with a person's money or emotions because you never know what will set them off. You may have some friends who will say, "Girl you don't have to like him; just get what you can from him." Well I'm here to tell you, that is a sure antidote for a butt whipping or worse...

Don't play with a person's feelings.

Stood Up...Craziest Excuses

My car broke down
My cousin had a heart attack
My mother was rushed to the hospital
I dropped my phone in the toilet
I ran out of gas
I had to baby-sit my little sister
I fell asleep
I got lost
I lost my cell phone
I was arrested
I fainted and had to be rushed to the hospital
I couldn't get a ride
My mom was tripping
I called you, but you didn't answer the phone
I had practice
My boys got me drunk
I didn't get my check
I had to work late
There was a fire on my street; no one could leave
The gate broke; I couldn't get my car out
My dad said no, stay home and study
My dog had babies
My friend had Super Bowl tickets
I was stuck in traffic
I had to go to my aunt's sister's friend's funeral
You had a bad attitude yesterday

Ladies, can you relate to any of the above? The nerve of these guys!

Remember that old saying...
Fool me once, shame on you! Fool me twice, shame on ME!

Get your Own Man

Don't go through life having to draw straws in your mind; wondering does he love you, or does he not? Will he leave her, or will he not?

As tempting as that man may be, don't let that man make a fool of you.

Honey, if you get involved with a married man, more than likely you will be on the losing end. Not too many married men will leave their wives for their girlfriends. That married man is thinking of the child support, the alimony, the house he may lose and the idea of starting all over from scratch is not too appealing. That old saying, "It's cheaper to keep her," came from a man.

Don't restrict yourself from possibly meeting the right guy because you are so tied down with the married one. Biblicaly, it is wrong to be with a married man; so don't cut your blessings short because of this guy who may just be using you for his extra curriculum. I was once told, a vagina has no face, and a penis has no conscious. Haven't you heard the laughter of some men who say, "...I would do her...just put a bag over her face?"

Don't be fooled by him always complaining about his wife. Saying how she is such a B----. Ask yourself; if the wife is as bad as he says, why does he continue to stay with her? Why have they just had another child, the vacation in the islands and what about the new car in the driveway? If a man is on his way out of the marriage, why is he still investing more and more into his home life?

Baby, for every front page, there is a back page. For every day, there's a night. That husband has his version and believe me the wife has hers. If he is telling you that she was so loving, kind and wonderful in the beginning, you have to wonder what made her go Sybil on him. Was it something he did to make her change completely?

Don't let your young age and lack of experience be the reason that you are taken advantage of by this mature, experienced and handsome man.

Oh my! You may have a boyfriend whose best friends are females. Most of the time, some men feel they can get along better with females then males.

He said they are just friends (she's like a sister to him); they are just kicking it together, and there is no romance involved.

Honey, he could be telling the truth; however, you have to ask yourself, can you handle this? Also, keep in mind; are you the one who has males as close friends (because you get along better with them)?

You both have to realize what's good for the goose is good for the gander. Don't dish out what you can't take.

Are you tired of always hearing her name mentioned?

You both need to communicate and determine what type of relationship you both want. Don't stress yourself out over this situation.

Again, did you know from the start what you were getting into? If the answer is yes, then don't blame him.

You are too young to be stressed behind any young man.

Chapter Two
Friends/Friends/ Friends

Friends

Don't use the word too easily. Remember, everyone that smiles in your face is not your friend. To have friends, you must also be a friend.

Some of the biggest challenges between mothers and daughters come about when friends enter the picture. Oh my God, we as mothers couldn't tell you anything. Hear you tell it, only your friends understand you. Yet you change friends as often as you change panties!

Falling in and out of friendships because you both bought the same outfit, or you both like the same guy, oh, and you heard she was talking about you behind your back.

True friends will be there through thick and thin. A friend is someone you can confide in, and who will give you constructive criticism, which you are open to accepting.

We have a lot of associates in life; however, be thankful if you can find one true and faithful friend (and never take them for granted).

We had a friend who had no family; but oh did she have good friends. She was a very loving and caring person; therefore, it was so easy to love her back.

When she passed away at home, she was found almost immediately. She was not like those you hear about who is found months after they died. And only then because of the mail piled high, or because of the smell coming through the windows.

When you love and are loved, people will check on you. They will go out of their way to make sure you're okay.

Be a friend...

It's Okay To Say No

Don't feel pressured into doing anything that you don't want to do. You will have some friends who will try and convince you to go somewhere or to do something that you really don't want to do.

If you're not feeling it, then don't do it. If you don't feel like having company, it's better to be honest, than allowing them to come over and you end up being rude to them.

Don't feel guilty for wanting alone time. And you really don't owe them a reason why you're saying no, but keep in mind - it's not what you say, but how you say it. There is no need to hurt their feelings.

Learn to take time for you.

Mom, Where Are All The Nice People?

Baby girl, there are still good people in the world. There are still people who know how to treat one another. You may have to be more selective of where you are meeting people. Believe me, morals and values are still being taught.

Don't lose faith in the human race; look at people individually. There is no perfect person, so try and look at the heart and soul of a person.

Never choose your friends because of their material or financial worth.

Treasure What You Have

Are you the back-up girl for your friends who are always calling to borrow something? I need your red dress, and it won't look nice unless I have your earrings (the ones you got for graduation).

You're always loaning out your things and getting them back raggedy or not getting them back at all. And what about your black sweater you loaned to Mary? She's a 38d and you're a 34b. Why would you loan her that sweater knowing her bazookas would stretch your good sweater out of shape?

What about the friend who needs to borrow your car because she was a little tipsy last week and wrecked her own? Honey; use common sense. If they can't take care of their own things, what makes you think they will take care of yours? And remember, cars run on gasoline, not on friendship and thank you. Be fair to each other, and don't take advantage of each other's kindness.

Don't try to buy friendships.

I Feel Sorry For Them

Sympathy is not a cure for those lacking motivation. Sometimes the school of hard knocks is what the person needs.

The longer you cradle a person, the more dependent they become. How will a person ever grow and be independent if everything is always done for them?

Honey, you can wipe a person's behind, and they will turn around and say you didn't wipe it good enough. You go and buy him a shirt, and he complains that you didn't buy the shoes to match.

What about the friend who you offered to pay for her manicure and she decides she wants a complete fill (with design tips)?

At some point you have to stop feeling sorry for them, and feel sorry for yourself for putting up with them.

You can give a man a fish, or you can give him a fishing pole and teach him how to fish (so he can feed himself for a lifetime).

Don't restrict yourself too much to a certain person or race. The real world is about mixture. Learn to adapt to whatever situation you're in. Don't ever feel less than someone just because you may not look or talk the way they do.

We are who we are and we can't hide from it. The world we live in is combined with all races. Whether at work, school or in the grocery store, we will interact at one time or another.

Look at people individually and fairly. Don't lump everyone in the same group. There is good and bad in every race, religion and sex.

Try and keep an open mind, because we truly can learn something from each other. Stop hating someone just because your friends may hate them. Keep in mind that hate is a strong word and emotion.

Honey, just because you think one way and someone else thinks another, doesn't make you or them wrong. It just means your opinions are different.

How can you point out the speck in someone else's eye, when there is a board in your own?

Well, They Were All Doing It

Why in the world did you spend all your money on that jacket? Your bills are due and you're out shopping for things you don't even need.

You said you didn't want to look like the odd ball. You wanted to save face, so you spent money you really didn't have.

Girl, you bought a fur jacket (and you don't even like fur), just because everyone else was doing it. Well, you better get comfortable wearing that jacket, because your disconnect bill from the gas company is sitting on your kitchen table.

Don't try and keep up with the Jones, Smiths or Tylers.

Don't over-buy when you can't afford to buy!

Birds Of A Feather

An apple doesn't fall far from the tree. Sometimes, you are judged by the people you associate with. This may not be fair, but it's true.

Honey, make wise decisions about those you choose as your running buddies. It's not always wise to hang with those who are always causing trouble, and those who are always drawing negative attention to themselves.

If you hang around a slut, you may be judged as a slut. The drug dealer named Pookey you're hanging with; guess what? People will think that you are also doing the same.

Sometimes you are guilty by association in people's eyes.

Why Can't You Be Like My Friends?

Simply because I'm your mother. I'm the one who cared for you. I'm the one who stayed up at night with you when you were sick. I'm the one who will give you my last penny, and not look for anything in return. And yes, I'm the one who wiped your behind then, and would wipe it now if need be.

Don't ever try and compare your mother and your friends, because there is no comparison. Most mothers would give up their lives to save yours!

Honey, don't bite off the hand that feeds you. I am your confidant, your supporter and your soldier in the midst of a battle. I am the one who loves you unconditionally.

I'm the one who tells you what you need to hear, and not just what you want to hear!

Chapter Three
Me, Myself and I

I Can Do What Pleases Me

Remember, what is done in the dark, will soon come to light. Have fun and enjoy life; however, have values and morals.

Be able to look yourself in the mirror and be proud of yourself. Honey, it may take twenty years, but your past will catch up to you (don't let it be a haunting one).

It's a very small world, and everybody knows somebody. Just because you feel grown and on your own, don't do things you may regret later on. Remember, use discretion and moderation; plus set boundaries for yourself.

Honey, it is not always what you do, but how you do it.

I Know I'm Cute

Well, who really thinks they're ugly? By right, you may be very beautiful, but honey, nothing lasts forever. In time, things go south and spread even worse. A lot of people are only a 12 pack of donuts away from being fat. One or two babies, and those hips can spread as easy as margarine.

Keep in mind that you may be oh so cute, but you can walk to the next block and see someone else that is fine as wine.

Don't get me wrong! Feel good about yourself, but never let your looks be the determination for your success. Beauty without brains and personality will be short-lived success.

God forbid you have a serious illness or accident, because this can change your appearance in a matter of a second. However, if you are a loving and kind person, people will always be in your corner, always willing to lend you a helping hand, willing to support you.

Don't let your beauty go to your head.

.

It's All About Me

Yea right!! Baby girl, it's no longer about you. You are no longer the Queen Bee. Things will no longer revolve around you and what you want.

Honey, you will have no one to pout to, and no one to make feel guilty for not giving you what you want. Remember when you used to close the door to your room and sulk? Well, you no longer have that door.

Your teachers, roommates and peers will look at you and say, "Honey, get a life," because they are going through their own drama, and could care less about yours.

Your cute little smile and your teary eyes will no longer move mountains for you.

Oh well, this is life!

Never Satisfied

If my nose was just a little smaller! And I would die for bigger breasts and a smaller butt. I always wanted green eyes; I'm buying my contacts this weekend. Once I get myself together, all I need is a boyfriend and my world will be complete.

Well young ladies, you can buy and change and change and buy, but those are only temporary fixes. Until you are happy within, you will always keep spending, trying to find happiness. Remember, material things are really just pacifiers.

Babe, you need to do some serious soul searching. Know that you are who God created and if someone has a problem with you, then it's their problem and tell them to take it up with God!

Learn to love what you have been blessed with, and get rid of the poor me attitude. Low self-esteem will allow people to step over and misuse you.

Learn to love yourself, because until you love you, how can you be good in any relationship or friendship?

Everybody Needs Somebody

Truly, no man is an island. You cannot live in this world and not need someone in your life. You can try and make yourself believe that all you need is yourself, but you are only fooling yourself.

Loneliness can be deadly. Everyone needs someone to laugh with, talk with and even cry with. Everyone needs a shoulder to lean on at one time or another. Whose hands are you holding during the Thanksgiving dinner (when it's time for the blessing)?

Have you ever wondered about the old lady at the bus stop with tons of bags? Where is her family? What about the man sleeping on the bus bench? Where are his friends? Were these people so mean and distant that their families and friends had given up on them?

Don't give up on people, and don't cause them to give up on you!

You're Not His Type

You are head over heels about this particular guy, but he doesn't even notice you. Your self-esteem has taken a dive, because he doesn't even know you're alive. You are now feeling down on yourself and your life.

Honey, believe me, just because you are not his type, doesn't mean you won't be the next guy's type. You have to learn that everyone has different likes and dislikes.

Some men like women with some meat on their bones, and some prefer the thin, sleek looking ones. Some like their women short; some like them tall. Some like short hair compared to long. Each guy has his own likening, and honey, every guy doesn't like big breasts.

Just like you have your preference (and feel no shame); they, too, have the right to have theirs. Hey, people like what they like.

Stop tripping. Someone will like you for you. Be cool; the right one will come along.

Excuses, Excuses, Excuses

Excuses are like butt holes, everybody has one! I would have, but; I should have, but; I could have, but.

How many times are you going to make excuses for not doing what you should have done? Ask yourself, did I really try as hard as I could have to complete what needed to be done?

Did I really care? Did I really want to? Did I really try my best? Also, ask yourself, did I really put my all and all into it? Was my heart really sincere?

If something went wrong in your trying, before you blame others, ask yourself, self, what could I have done differently?

Be accountable for your actions or lack thereof. You may not succeed at everything you try, but be proud in knowing you gave it your best!

Chapter Four
Reality Check

Too Many Rules At This House

No entry before 9:00 a.m.
No shirt, no shoes, no service
No pets allowed
No smoking
Etc., etc., etc...

They all sound like rules, don't they?

You couldn't wait to leave home because you didn't like having to follow rules; yet everywhere you go, there are rules to follow. Whether you're at school, work or just in your favorite store, there are rules.

If you don't show up for work, you will be fired. Miss too many classes, you will be dropped. Don't pay your cell phone bill, it will be shut off!

No matter how much money you have or don't have, you will always have rules to follow. And believe me, once you leave this house, you will see that the rules at home weren't all that bad!

The only difference with rules is, those with money sometimes have the power of making some of the rules. So if you want to be the "Big Wig" making the rules, go to school, get your education and you may just be one of the rule makers.

Ground Rules

Yes, those doggone rules again! You have a roommate now and things are getting rough. You both started off with good intentions, but something went very wrong. You both should have created a contract between yourselves and set some rules.

Rules, consideration and respect must be a part of any relationship, especially when you are sharing a place with someone. That perfect situation can turn sour because of inconsideration and lack of respect.

Ladies, you must also be willing to compromise, and keep in mind that there are some lines that you just don't cross.

You definitely need trust in one another. Remember, the company you bring to your place will not only affect you, but also your roommate. Never loan out your key to your place, because you are giving up your privacy. Don't be too quick letting someone move in, because you may have hell getting them out!

In a perfect world, those living together would be as close as two peas in a pod; however, this is the real world and problems do occur. Keep the lines of communication open. Something as simple as you wearing her blouse can piss her off; or her using your hairbrush may send you through the ceiling.

Keep others out of your business and out of your problems. If you see things are not going to get any better, maybe it's time for someone to move, (and remember, change those locks).

Be Careful What You Ask For

Mom, I want a tall, good-looking guy with money. And I know I want a job paying me at least six figures.

Sometimes we restrict ourselves by limiting ourselves. We often get hooked on wanting a certain person or thing, and refusing to accept other than that. Honey, know that accepting less than we desire does not necessarily mean settling for less.

Instead of wanting a man that is 6'0 and built, maybe you should go for that man who is 5'6, medium built, nice, honest and hard working. And girls, be careful of a man that stays in the mirror longer than you (ha-ha).

You may want that six-figure paying job, but you may have to start off midway until you accomplish your goals. And you better be prepared to handle the responsibilities that come with that high paying job.

Mom, I'm Grown, But I Need

You leave home saying you are grown, but every two weeks you're calling for money. Either you need money to buy clothes, pay your utilities or just money to buy groceries.

When you get tired of calling mom, you sneak and call daddy – asking for money to get gas for your car, and your cell phone bill.

Honey, after the fifth call in a month, we finally tell you that you're going to have to manage your finances better.

Now you're mad and too proud to call home for help (even though you are barely surviving). Well, baby, don't have too much pride. We all need help at one time or another, but don't make a habit of begging.

If you are always coming with your hand held out, people will run from you. They'll see your name appear on the caller I.D., and will ignore the call. Shhhh... be quiet, I think she's at the front door.

At some point you have to ask yourself what you could do differently to make your money last longer. At another point, you may even have to explore ways of earning extra money.

Don't Blame Me

Okay, things aren't going right in your life. It seems like everything you have tried has turned out wrong. When I call you, I get instant attitude. You want to blame someone other than yourself, so you blame me. Well, honey, I'm not the one.

Baby girl, accept the responsibility of your actions and decisions. I tried to guide and direct you, but you felt I was all in your business. You reminded me that you were no longer a child, and to let you live your life.

Well, it's time for you to reevaluate some things. Rethink your decisions and learn to let go of your stubbornness and pride. It's okay to ask for help.

We often attack and blame those that are closest to us.
Honey, learn who's on your side!

What's Your Pleasure?

If you don't have a hobby, find one. So often, we hear that a person needs to get a life! Whether it's reading, exercising or dancing, have a passion in life.

Have something to look forward to; something that makes you smile. Pleasures in life make living so much nicer.

Remember, all work and no play makes for a boring day. Have a balance in your life.

Be well-rounded.

I'm Still Finding Myself

Please don't be 30 and still finding yourself. At some point in your life, you have to settle down and start accomplishing something. College may not be for everyone, but a job better be!

No grown person should be living at home (with parents) and not working or going to school. At some point, you have to realize that your free loading days are over. I would love to know how someone 30 years old lives for free unless they are living off someone.

Just like you realized there was no tooth fairy, and that no fat man in a red suit would be coming down the chimney, you have got to realize that you have to be responsible for you! Hell, I'm at the age where you may have to help me (ha-ha).

Think about it! How many people really love their job (or like working period)? Most people are just trying to stay afloat.

Even the Bible says, "A Man That Does Not Work, Does Not Eat." Wow, can you imagine that?

A Day Late, A Dollar Short

Don't put off tomorrow what you can do today. So many people have missed out on blessings because of laziness and because of taking things for granted.

Many people assume they have all the time in the world to do what needs to be done. Just like the perm left on your head too long can break off your hair, or the food cooked too long will burn. Honey, know that taking too long can be costly.

As I said before, take care of business first. Don't sit around always using the excuse that you are waiting for the perfect time. Sometimes you have to make it the perfect time.

Remember how you lost out on the free trip; how you missed out on the free money, and how you waited too late to get the classes you wanted?

Baby girl, remember, time waits on no one.

Secrets

Secrets can destroy lives. So many families have been torn apart because of lies and secrets.

So many people are in therapy, mental hospitals and on medications, because of family secrets.

Be true in all you do. Secrets cause pain, distrust and confusion, along with a thousand why's.

Don't ever let your child have to wonder who their father is. What happened to the sister that left home and never came back? Don't let them have to wonder why they look different from their siblings.

Why was there whispering going on at Christmas dinner when cousin Sue walked through the door? In the past, a lot of older people believed, let sleeping dogs lie; or the old saying, "Leave well enough alone." However, this theory has come back to bite so many people in their behinds.

The best kept secret is one that never occurred.

Try and live your life secret free.

Society will care for our elderly and the young. There are programs and funds available for the little ones who are too young to take care of themselves. The elderly are respected and cared for because they have paid their dues. If you are mentally challenged, you may get lucky and reap some benefits.

However, when you are young and able, you are expected to carry your own load. A lot of free programs have been cut because of budget cuts. As time goes on, more and more free programs may be a thing of the past.

Believe it or not, you as a young and healthy person are expected to work and provide for yourself. The government is ending those free rides of living off the fat of the land.

You may think that fast food jobs are not rewarding. The janitorial job may not be too appealing either! However, the government feels a job is a job. We all had to start somewhere. When handouts are given, remember, you won't be on the most needed list, but on the forgotten list.

Remember, there is nothing like having your own money!

TMI (Too Much Information)

Yea, I already know what you're thinking! Why am I telling you all this when you are only 17? You feel that none of this has anything to do with you.

Well, guess what? You're wrong. You need to know about everything in this book and even more. You think you're grown, but honey just wait until you get out there in the real world on your own.

It's best that you listen and learn now, so you will set the path you want to follow. Honey, it's never too early to build self-esteem. It's never too early to learn about giving respect and expecting respect; and it's surely never too early to learn about appreciating life!

At your age, learning will only make you wiser and stronger.

Have an open mind. You may not agree with everything I wrote; however, I bet you will learn something.

Chapter Five
The Mighty Green

Money, Money, Money

Get your education and go for the gusto! Never depend on anyone else to pave the way for you.

There is nothing worse than having to hear someone constantly say, "If it wasn't for me, you wouldn't have anything!"

Just like you want someone with something to offer, don't you think he is thinking the same way? Money equals money.

So often, women stay stuck in relationships because they can't make it on their own financially.

Money Don't Grow On Trees

Don't spend every penny you have. As sure as the sky is high and the ground is low, emergencies will come. Don't make a habit of borrowing what you can't pay back, and don't loan what you can't afford to give away.

Platinum, gold or bronze, don't do it! It may look cool to flash that credit card in front of your friends, but believe me, you are asking for trouble.

Don't leave college owing as much on your credit cards as you do on your education. Debt and bills can keep you depressed. Living pay check to pay check is not a way to live. Don't have to rob Peter to pay Paul.

Take care of your money as if you have no one else to depend on but you!

Broke, But Still Enjoying Life

You're broke and bored! Well, learn to have fun when you don't have money. Don't sit around moping about the fact that you can't have a nice weekend because you don't have any money. There is an entire world out there for you to explore and enjoy. Try enjoying some of these simple and free things in life.

Skating
Bike Riding
Hiking
Manicure-pedicure girl's day at home
Play cards or games
Take a walk in the park
Potluck dinner with friends
Free concert in the park
Visit a bookstore
Visit old friends/family
Go to the beach
Start a book club with friends
Look for free events in the calendar section of the newspaper
Attend church activities
Exercise with friends at each other's homes
Volunteer work
Become a fan at the neighborhood school games

Fun doesn't always have to cost money.

Bad Credit

If nothing else follows you, your credit history does. Whether good or bad, you make the decision. One day you will want to buy that new car, or that house; even something as small as the new couch you saw the other day.

Well, honey, if your credit is bad, you will get reject after reject. Remember when you didn't pay your cell phone bill and you ignored the collection letters. It will show as a negative on your credit rating.

Maintain your good credit because it can make or break you. Develop a positive payment history. And just because someone offers you a credit card, you don't have to accept it. Too much credit can be a negative also.

If all those shoes, purses and clothes have gotten you in debt, go visit a credit counselor for help.

Periodically, have your credit report sent to you. Check for errors on your report and make sure you compare the social security numbers.

It's a good idea to check with several credit bureaus. If you notice there are errors, make sure you follow up with letters to the credit bureau and to the companies reporting the negative report. Create a filing system for your business and keep it up-to-date.

Treasure your social security number and your other personal information because someone can destroy your good name and credit if you don't.

One of the safest and easiest ways to manage your money is through a checking account. This is an easy way of paying and keeping track of what you have paid for. By paying with a check, you have a permanent record of payment if it ever comes into question. You should keep a record (register) of money spent, which will help you develop a budget. Keep in mind some banks charge a monthly checking account fee (as well as check reorder fee).

Always use ink when writing your check so that no one can change your numbers. Print and write your numbers clearly to alleviate any misunderstandings. Do not change the way you sign your name. If you make a mistake on a check, write VOID on the check and use the next one.

When using the ATM, don't forget to subtract any funds taken from your account, and add any that are deposited into your account. ***WORD OF CAUTION***, be careful when using the ATMs (robberies do occur at them).

Eventually you will need to learn the difference between:
Social Security taxes
Employment taxes
Unemployment taxes
Income taxes
Sales tax
Property taxes

If you own a vehicle, you should have car insurance, so learn the following:

Bodily injury liability
Property damage liability
Medical payment insurance
Uninsured motorist protection
Comprehensive physical damage insurance

Learn the difference between Term Life Insurance and Universal Life Insurance.

If you're the type to venture into business deals, learn about:
Common Stocks
Corporate Bonds
U. S. Treasury Bonds
Municipal Bonds
Preferred Stocks
IRAs

Learn ways of investing so your money will grow for you.

Where there is a will, there's a way. Don't be too quick to give up on the idea of going to college, because it can be within your reach.

Start early, networking and obtaining information on scholarships and grants. Believe me, there is money available; however, you will need to do some research in finding it.

Talk with your school counselors, search bookstores and the Internet on locating funds that are available.

Keep in mind, in order to be awarded these scholarships, you have to have something to offer. Learn to be the best writer you can, because you will (most likely) be asked to write an essay. The better the essay, the better your chance of winning.

Participate in social events. Give back to the community by doing volunteer work. Go for the whole enchilada. Have the best GPA you can. Scholarships are given to the students with the highest GPA.

Did you know that even playing an instrument might be the key to opening that door to college?

Chapter Six
Self Preservation

To Thine Own Self Be True

Sometimes it has to be all about you! Ask yourself, self, am I happy and at peace? If the answer is no, then it's time to make some serious changes.

People will be shocked, wondering what is happening to you, but they will get over it. Life is too short to be unhappy. Living is not about being depressed and unhappy all the time. You may have to let go of some people and some things in order to be at peace with yourself.

Remember, it's not your job to please everyone (and you never could anyway). Be good to yourself and stop trying to carry everyone's burden.

Be thankful for your life and the ability to live it.

Straight up, people will do to you what you allow them to do. If you see that someone is disrespecting and misusing you, put a stop to it immediately. The longer you let it drag on, the harder it will be for you to stop it.

Don't walk around with the word, "Fool" written on your forehead. You can't demand love, but you can demand respect. If you continue to allow someone to use you as their doormat, they will.

Ask the question, if I did to them what they are doing to me, would they accept it? (I doubt it).

Remember, the door swings both ways, and don't let it be a revolving one. If a person can't treat you the way you deserve to be treated, kick them to the curb. Let the doorknob hit them where the good Lord split them.

Don't be fooled by letting this person in and out of your life. Look at the sincerity of a person's heart.

Naive And Gullible

Keep your eyes and ears open. Don't believe everything someone tells you. Learn to research things for yourself. Honey, remember, everything that glitters ain't gold.

Anyone can brag and tell lies, so listen and evaluate the person doing the talking. You will find those who will talk out of both sides of their mouth, agreeing with whatever is convenient.

The word naive means to have lack of worldly wisdom, and the word gullible means to be easily tricked or cheated. Don't be anyone's fool. You need to have common sense, along with book sense.

And ladies, please don't confuse common sense with God's sense. Many a mistake has been blamed on God. Those who say, "The Lord told me to quit my job." Oh and, "I know John is going to be my husband, because the Lord told me so." Now why would the Lord tell you that when John is already married to Tanya?

Think smart...

Wake Up

Nothing comes to a sleeper but a dream! Don't just dream, but chase your dreams. Make goals and go into action making them work. You may not reach all your goals, but you will never know till you try. And think about what all you will have learned and experienced in trying.

Be realistic in your goals, and don't be in denial about the reality of a situation. Have a Plan B (even a C), and never put all your eggs in one basket.

Don't give up too easily. Mental defeat can be your worst enemy.

Think positive
Think survivor
Think winner

School Takes Too Long

What else do you have to do with your time? Especially if you are single and have no kids, take advantage of getting your education.

Back in the day, your parents may have excelled by having good jobs with little education, but things have changed. That same job your parents have, are now requiring that you have a college degree.

Competition is greater now. You have to have more to offer than your competitor who is battling for the same job you want.

Remember, knowledge is power. Education and determination are the keys to success. Read and be willing to learn.

So many students have been sent home from college because they took their eyes off the prize. Stay focused, go to class and get your education!

Simplify Your Life

Learn to make life easy on yourself. Get organized and get rid of the clutter in your life.

Use your weekends to your advantage. Cook a big Sunday dinner that will last you for a few days. This will help keep you from having to cook during the week, or eating out so much. Eating out is not as healthy and it is definitely more expensive. Learn to freeze your leftovers and have them for dinner in a couple of weeks or months.

Turn on some good music or your favorite weekend program and iron your clothes for the week. You will be surprised how much time that will save you during the week. It will even allow you to sleep longer or exercise a little before you start your day.

Super, regular or premium, fill your car up on the weekend. Again, this will save you extra time during the week.

Create a list of things to do, and if possible do some of them on your lunch break. Whether you study, pay some bills or just rest your eyes, create a system for yourself.

Keep your life as stress free as possible, because emergencies do pop up.

Safety First

Go out in groups if you can. If you leave together, you come home together. If you are going on a blind date, make sure someone knows the 411 on this guy. Also, watch that Internet hookup! Anyone can seem nice while typing.

When that new date is coming over, never let him know you're alone. Let him believe your brother, sister or friend is in the next room.

Honey, always know your whereabouts. If you're being followed, never go home; go to an open business (where people are).

If you are in the midst of a crime, holler fire! People are quicker to respond to someone hollering fire, than hollering for help (how sad). On that hot summer night, don't sleep with those windows open; buy a fan.

Don't ever think you are above anything. There are numerous people dead because they took things for granted, assuming nothing would ever happen to them.

Think smart; be cautious.

As sure as the sky is high, things just happen. We can either look at life like the glass is either half empty or half full.

Some things we will never understand why they happen, so we have to look to the Lord to give us understanding.

Life can be sweet, but we have to learn to deal with the bitter as well. Life is no bed of roses, but learn to smell them when you can.

Learn to appreciate the little things in life, because honey, there is someone somewhere who's worse off than you!

Remember the story of the man feeling sorry for himself? He complained about the raggedy shoes he wore, until he walked upon the man who had no feet.

Learn to count your blessings!

Who Will Understand The
Importance Of My Flight,,,
Quote By: Courtney Hayes
(17 years old).

Chapter Seven
Be of Good Character

Hey Lady, Do You Have A Quarter?

Give a helping hand to someone. Whether it's the transient on the street or the old lady at the bus stop. Reach out to someone.

You may not be the type to go and sit with the sick at a hospital. You may be the type to volunteer teaching an adult to read. If you are blessed with any measure of strength, help someone that is less fortunate.

By helping someone else, your heart will feel happy; you may even catch yourself smiling. Helping someone less fortunate will make you realize how blessed you are.

That pair of boots you wanted just doesn't seem that important after you have just fed a child who hadn't eaten in a week.

Give a helping hand.

Drugs & Alcohol

Run, baby, run! These things will alter your personality. They will make you do things you would never have dreamed of doing. Hell, you might wake up one morning with Big Bubba lying next to you, and you wonder, oh my God, did I sleep with this slob?

When you're intoxicated, you can easily be taken advantage of, and what a price to pay. Always have control of yourself and your actions. Remember, for every action, there is a reaction.

Oh yea, when you're out, don't leave your drink unattended. Anyone at any given time can easily slip something in your drink. And before you know it, you have been drugged and taken for a ride that you will never forget. Many young ladies have been raped after drugs were slipped in their drinks,when they simply turned their heads (for a quick second).

Drugs and alcohol can and do kill. They can kill you, and those you love!

Pain In The Butt

There is nothing worse than having a loved one with a drug or alcohol habit. They will curse you, call you everything but a child of God, and the next day tell you how much they love you.

You love this person, yet you are embarrassed by them, not knowing how they will act at any given time. Never knowing what frame of mind they will be in, therefore, you are reluctant to invite them over.

Don't be this type of person, always having to be excluded from the family parties. Believe me, these vices will change your entire personality, where you won't even recognize yourself.

Please, please, please - get help for yourself. Do it for you, and do it for those you say you love.

God Don't Like Ugly

Do unto others, as you would have them do unto you! Treat people the way you want to be treated.

If someone does you wrong, don't waste your energy and time trying to pay them back, because they will get theirs in the end. They may need a cold glass of water from you one day.

Don't go tit for tat with people, because it's not worth it. And two wrongs really don't make it right.

Don't lose sleep, get depressed and not eat because of what someone has done or said to you.

Remember, "Vengeance is mine," said the Lord!

Time And Place For Everything

Yes, the Lord says come as you are; however, use some discretion! Don't go to church the same way you would go to the club.

Put a shawl or sweater over that halter dress. If you don't have one, borrow one, just like you would borrow something to wear to that party on Friday night.

That thong with your shear dress should not be worn to church. Your butt cheeks should not be seen clapping as hard as your hands are clapping.

It is one thing not to know any better, but if you honestly know better, don't come to church dressed in attire to feed your need for attention.

Honey, please don't be nasty. Remember the adage, "Cleanliness Is Next To Godliness."

You probably thought when you moved that you would only clean when you felt like it. Well that is just being lazy.

Please be considerate of your roommate and those who may just stop by to visit. Believe me, if you have company at your place and it's nasty, they will wonder how you must keep your personal hygienes as well.

These same people may be reluctant to even eat anything you cook. Life will be so much easier and simpler if you are clean and organized.

Clutter adds confusion.

Material Girl

Mom, thanks for the birthday gifts, but you know I only like to wear Old Navy, Roca Wear and Fubu!

The nerve of these girls! No job, no money, and they have the nerve to be picky. Whatever happened to thank you?

Girls, be thankful for whatever you get (especially when it's free). And ladies, clothes don't make the person.

You can have on a $20.00 outfit and look like a $100.00. Or you can have on a $100.00 outfit and look like $20.00. However, if you are neat and clean, you can wear it looking like a $1,000.00.

Everything does not have to be name brand to look nice...

She Won't Amount To Anything

You will find in life that everyone may not be happy for you. Unfortunately, jealousy is alive and in full force. Some people are hoping that you fail, because they failed.

Some people are envious and bitter, hating to see others accomplish success in life, because they feel they weren't dealt the same hand.

There may be some just hoping and waiting to see you mess up. Honey, some have already concluded that you will never amount to anything. They have assumed you will be buck wild (loose) once you get out on your own.

Others have concluded that you will be knocked up (pregnant) with two or three babies by the time you turn 21.

Baby, don't go out like that. Prove these people wrong. Work hard, and fight hard to accomplish your goals. Strive to be the best that you can be in life.

You owe no one but you! Make yourself proud of you.

Attitude Is Everything

Girl, the right attitude, plus a kick butt personality can take you a long way. That personality of yours can either make or break you!

Stop the negative persona. Learn to smile. Learn to communicate. Haven't you noticed how some people look so mean, you hate to even speak to them? Some will give you that evil look, "Don't even look my way!"

However, I have seen personalities that will light up a room. I've seen people get jobs, just because of their warm and gentle spirit and personality. And no, this doesn't mean you are kissing up, it just means that you know how to work it, and girl work it to your advantage.

Stop looking mean. Stop throwing out that "don't mess with me" attitude. Believe it or not, smiling even makes you feel better.

It takes more effort and energy to frown than to smile!

Sleep With One Eye Open

Watch what you do in life. If you're doing what you know is wrong, you better sleep with one eye open.

If you do the crime, you will do the time. What is done in the dark, will soon come to light.

Don't want something so bad in life that you are willing to stoop too low to get it. Ask yourself, how low will I go? Don't live your life wondering if "they" are coming! Don't have the shakes every time you see a police car, or hear a siren. There is nothing worse than living in fear, and nothing greater than living in peace.

Maintain morals, honesty and integrity. There is nothing worth going to jail for. There is nothing worse than wondering if so and so is coming to pay you back for what you did to them.

Live Good - Sleep Good!

Goodie Two Shoes

From day one, you have been following the straight path. You were often teased for being the good little girl. You were always the responsible, trustworthy and right-on- time person.

Everyone knew they could depend on you (no matter what), and you're tired of it. You often wondered what it would be like to say, "The hell with everyone and everything." You are just tired of feeling used.

Baby girl, know there are rewards in store for you. Your good deeds will not go unnoticed. Keep in mind, they may not even be noticed by those you helped most. Your rewards may not come when you want them to, but they will come at the right time.

Honey, because of you being you, someone has survived; someone has been able to smile again. You probably fed someone that had no clue where their next meal was coming from. You have encouraged someone to keep on trying in life, and you have lifted their spirits.

Remember the single mother who said, if not for her child, she would have given up on life? Or the mother who feels her child is what made her determined to change her lifestyle?

You, too, have been that extended mother to someone. You are the type of person that someone wants in their corner.

Honey, be who you are.

Single With Child

Take care of that baby. You chose to be a mother, so be a good one!

Does this mean you have to change your priorities? Yes, it does! Does this mean you have to make sacrifices? Yes, it does!

Don't ever put someone before your child. If you meet the guy of your dreams and he can't accept you and your child, tell him to step on.

And ladies, please don't meet a guy one week and the next week he is baby-sitting your child. You don't know enough about this man yet.

And please make me understand how you kicked the father of the child to the curb, because he didn't have an excellent job, yet you allow the new guy (with no job) and a drug habit into your child's life? Where is the common sense in that?

Listen to and notice your child. If your child seems nervous, stressed or unhappy when around certain people (men or women), just maybe there is something going on behind your back. Check it out!

Special Note If you are new to an area, go to your nearest Police Station and check for possible Sex Offenders in your area (Megan's Law). Simply, put in your address!

What If Everybody Was Like Me?

One day, ask yourself, "If everyone in this world was like me, what type of world would this be?"

When you are finding faults in others, take a good hard look at yourself. Are you a fair, caring and honest person? Are you a true friend?

Think about your moodiness, selfishness and your hot temper! Are you an enjoyable person to be around?

After you have answered these questions honestly and the answers are no, then maybe it's time to do an attitude adjustment.

Never ever ask someone to do something that you are not willing to do in return.

Stop The Madness

Are you one of those people who are always looking for someone to blame for your life? Some people are still holding grudges because they didn't get the pair of skates promised to them when they were ten. And they drink and do drugs because their dad was always working and never made it to their games.

Oh, and they blame their weight problem on the mother who gave them cookies and milk at night when they were five years old (forget the fact they are now 20). And they hate the world because their uncle called them chubby cheeks.

Girl, we all have a past history of disappointments and negative things said or done to us at one time or another. However, at some point you have to move on. You have to learn to let go of the hatred and ill feelings you are holding towards life and others.

If you need counseling, then get it. Reality is the longer you harbor hatred, bitterness and negativity, you are only keeping yourself from progressing.

It's time to stop the cycle.

Oh my, the attention seeker. Are you always the victim; always needing someone to come to your rescue?

If you really need help, ask for it! However, don't always be the damsel in distress, because after a while people will hide from you!

Don't be the drama queen. Stop making a big thing out of everything, and keep things in perspective.

Why Lie?

Truly, honesty is the best policy. Once you lie, it's easy to keep lying.

Don't live your life as a lie, because once you lie about something, you have to constantly remember what you said, trying not to be caught in your lies.

Let your word be your bond. Again, it's not what you say, but how you say it. Don't lie just to tell people what they want to hear.

So many lies are told trying to impress others. Honey, either people will like you for who you are, or they won't.

If people consider you a liar, it will be very difficult for anyone to ever believe you. One day, you may honestly be telling the truth, but who would believe you?

Ask yourself, was that lie really necessary?

Hush Your Mouth

Sometimes it's best to be thought a fool, than to speak and remove all doubt!

Ladies, sometimes it's best to be quiet and be still. Learn that you don't always have to get in the last word.

Remember, everyone has their own opinions. Words can't be taken back, so be careful what you say.

Silence can be golden. Be slow to anger, slow to wrath.

Everything you think should not always be said!

Think before you speak.

Stop The Gossip

Words hurt and can't be taken back. People have been killed for gossiping and because of gossip. We need to go back to that old saying; if you have nothing nice to say about a person, then don't say anything at all!

We as women have the greatest problem keeping a secret. How many times have you been told something in confidence, and before the phone lines cooled off, you're already on the phone telling someone else?

A lesson to us all! If you don't want something repeated, don't tell it. That wagging tongue is a troublemaker.

Remember, whatever gossip you are hearing is probably half the truth and there are two sides to every story (maybe even three).

I Want To Be Like You

Somewhere, someone is watching you! Some young child may be watching what you do and how you do it.

Honey, you are at the age where kids may be looking up to you as their role model or mentor. There are younger kids who need direction and guidance, and you may just be the one to do it.

Whether it's the way you dress, talk or walk, someone is looking at you and saying, "I want to be like you when I grow up." All role models are not those seen on television or in the movies.

As you were taught, you are now at the age of teaching. You can motivate and encourage someone to be the best they can be. You should be telling that younger child how they can succeed in life if they continue to try.

It's time for you to reach and teach someone. It's time for you to set a positive example.

There is a young child that needs a smile, a hug, or just a thumbs up! You are that person to do it.

Just A Simple Word

I love you, thank you, I'm proud of you, or please forgive me can mean so much.

Often times, people just need to hear some encouraging words. Stop saying things like, I hate you, you're ugly, or you are no good. Try wishing someone a good day!

Remember that old saying, if you can't say something nice, then don't say anything at all?

You're beautiful, or your hair looks nice, can lift someone's spirits. Telling someone they have great potential has just motivated that young man or lady to keep trying at their schoolwork.

Speak positive words.

Cool Your Temper

Stop being so aggressive and angry. You cursed the driver out who drove too close to your car.

The cashier that was new and too slow pissed you off. What is all this anger about? Learn to take some deep breaths and count to ten if you have to. You just never know who's who!

Remember the lady you gave the finger to? Well, what if she is the dentist that may be pulling your teeth next week; or the young man you cursed at yesterday could very well be the boss at the job you are applying for.

Oh, and the guy you mooned is the Minister of the Youth Group at church. Watch who you're showing your ass to!

Just like you have a temper, you may just run into someone who has a worse one. Police officers are not the only ones carrying a gun.

Don't get yourself into a situation that you can't get out of. Remember, there is always someone tougher than you.

Chapter Eight
Thinking Smart

Party, Party, Party

Kick your heels up and have fun! However, be selective and know that you can't attend every party!

Take care of business first. It doesn't take a rocket scientist to understand that if you have a final tomorrow, you should stay home and study! Believe me, if you miss that one party, there will be another one the very next week (or day).

Parties have always been around and they will always be around. Be selective in your choices. Don't put yourself in unnecessary danger.

If there are drugs at the location, leave. If the location is not kosher, get to stepping.

Don't put yourself in harm's way just because you want to party!

Take care of your body and your appearance. Don't walk around looking unkept and nasty. From the top to the bottom, clean every crevice on you. Open wide; not just your mouth, but your tail as well.

Honey, there is nothing worse than a funky woman. Don't you dare walk around smelling like Charlie Tuna. Every now and then you may have to switch up and try a different deodorant or mouthwash. It doesn't hurt to carry some extra panties, wipes and shields in your purse.

If you are feeling a little concerned about your body odor, ask a friend, "Girl, am I musty? Do I need a mint? Or, is the track in my weave showing?

If we as friends can't be honest with each other, then who can we depend on? Why is it that we can have a booger in our nose, and no one will tell us?

Girl, make sure you keep a mirror in your purse at all times.

Care about your appearance. Even when you are feeling down, fix yourself up; it will make you feel better.

What Is That You Have On?

Honey, everybody can't wear everything; or should I say, everybody should not wear everything! Just because something is in style, doesn't mean you should wear it.

Haven't you ever seen someone out and you ask yourself, "Why in the world didn't her family tell her she is too big for that outfit?" Baggy clothing may be in style, but if you are a size 1 wearing clothes a size 12, you will look like an anorexic reject.

And believe me, you can be sexy without having to show everything. Don't make yourself a sexual assault victim. It is a proven fact that more sexual crimes occur during the summer months because of the risqué clothing worn by ladies.

Piercing and tattoos should be done in moderation. One day when you are applying for that high paying job and your body art is overpowering your skills and knowledge, that boss will direct you to the nearest clown audition.

It may not be fair, but we are judged by our appearance. The first impression you give, may be the only one you ever have a chance to give.

Remember, there is a time and place for everything.

Check Them Out!

Every night of the week you are looking at the music videos. When you get tired of looking at those, you switch to one of your favorite sitcoms.

Your nose is wide open, thinking your life could and should be that way. You have decided that you want to look just like the girl on the show. You have concluded that your boyfriend will start acting and treating you like the guy in the movies treats his lady.

Your mind is made up! You want to have what you've seen on television and in the movies. Honey, this is not reality...come back down to earth.

Don't ever try and pattern yourself after the movies, videos and shows. Keep in mind, these are actors and actresses playing a role. Make sure your goals are your goals and not someone else's.

Remember, Jeanie really didn't live in a bottle, and Gilligan didn't own any island!

Baby, learn to take care of your health. You have medical coverage, so use it. Don't take your health for granted. I used to be the one refilling your prescriptions; however, it's now your responsibility, so handle it.

The one excuse, "I don't like the way that medication tastes," will no longer work. Honey, it's not about taste, it's about what will make you feel better. Let go of some of the junk food. You are young, but you need to eat a balanced diet. Eat food with substance, because when you're sick, that same substance will help you bounce back quickly.

And pleeeeeeeease, when it's 20 degrees and pouring down rain, don't wear those cute blue sandals because they match your cute little dress. Use your head, and put some shoes on your feet. Oh, and I know you don't want to wear a jacket, because it will wrinkle your outfit, but girl, use the brains the good Lord gave you.

Chapter Nine
Be Prepared

Nine To Five Is Not My Style

Some people can't imagine punching a time clock, or having to start work the same time every day. If you're this type of person, you better think creatively! Think - I'll be my own boss.

Start researching different jobs and careers that are productive. You may have to take some courses in order to gain some skills. When deciding what type of job or business you would be good at, also think about your lifestyle.

Are you a budget shopper, or do you wear only name brand clothing? Are you content living in an apartment or is a home your desire? What about that economy car, or do you prefer the big luxury smooth ride?

You have to decide what job will allow you to live the lifestyle you are accustomed to, or plan to become accustomed to. Are you a Latte type of girl, or would the cup of coffee from the neighborhood market do just fine?

If you've concluded that you have to be your own boss and have your own thing going on, think of some of the following self-initiated careers.

Photographer (always needed)
Day Care/Elder Care Center
Janitorial Company
Real Estate Agent, Loan Officer, Appraiser
Notary
Painter
Wedding Planner/Coordinator
Hair Stylist
Landscaper

Think positive and do your research; there are so many doors to open.

It's Between Me And The New Guy

Things have improved in the working world for women, but we still have further to go. I have stressed education to you because females are still having to prove they are worthy of some jobs.

A lot of companies would rather hire a man versus a woman; however, when you enter the interview with a degree and/or outstanding credentials, they will have to sit up and take notice.

In the past, many women were overlooked for jobs simply because they were female, females with issues that companies felt would prevent them from doing their jobs.

Companies wanted and needed employees that would produce. They feared hiring women because women often call in sick because of cramps, feeling bloated, PMS, pregnant or morning sickness. Women are usually the ones calling in sick with the new baby, the baby's check up, and day care problems. We have a bad hair day, but we call in, saying a sore throat.

All of the above are a part of a female's life. Yet, in the work place, some male bosses may not be sensitive to these issues, even though they may have a wife, sister or aunt with the same issues.

Most supervisors don't want to hear that you didn't get much sleep last night because Johnnie had a bad dream.

So ladies, make sure you have something to offer that employer, something greater than your male competition.

My Big Interview

Today is the day for your job interview and you're nervous. You have decided to wear your little red dress (and I do mean little) with no stockings (because it's too hot).

Are you crazy? Unless you are interviewing for a cocktail waitress, you put on some stockings and wear something more conservative. Again, there is a time and place for everything.

Remember, this is your first impression, so learn to dress according to the position you are applying for. Believe me, if you are dressed a notch above the others, you will stand out in the boss' mind (when he's making his decision).

Also, take time and prepare yourself for the interview. Stand in front of the mirror and practice speaking. Do your homework by finding out as much as you can about the job you're applying for. Don't walk into that interview unprepared.

Dress to impress, and be prepared.

Chapter Ten
Stop The Negativity

Misery Loves Company

Oh my God! You will run into people who never have anything good to say. They are never positive about anything. You can say good morning and they will say, "What's so good about it?" Honey, don't hang around these people too long, because they will drag you down.

Look for positive, good-spirited friends - those who have a love for life.

If you know someone who is always poor me, look at them and wonder why they're always the victim. And definitely be careful seeking advice from those who are always negative.

Some people are always saying, "If I were you, I wouldn't," but nine times out of ten, they would!

Think positive; be positive.

When you see someone who's got it together; ask them how they did it. Find out what motivated and encouraged them. I bet they would be more than willing to help a sista out!

Honey, don't block your blessing because of jealousy and envy. When you are fortunate enough to know or meet someone who has succeeded in life, seek their advice and wisdom.

Keep in mind that everyone has to start from somewhere. Even if you are born with a silver spoon in your mouth, at some point you better obtain the knowledge and wisdom of maintaining what you have. Remember, it's easy to fall from riches to rags.

Even those who may have failed at a task can teach you something! They can teach you how not to make the same mistakes they did.

Learn to appreciate what you can learn from others.

I'm Quitting

You have made up your mind that you don't have to take anything from anyone! You were constantly late for work and got tired of your boss giving you negative stares, so you decided to just quit.

Your teacher refused to give you an extension on turning in your report, so you quit the class. You disliked the assistant track coach, so you quit the track team.

Wake up! This is the real world and you better realize it fast. You cannot keep quitting, just because you don't get your way. Know that there is no perfect anything in life. If you think you can continue to quit on things, you are quitting on life.

If you think you are going to walk out on every situation that is not done to your satisfaction, you are living in a fantasy world.

You have to pay your dues in life just like everyone else.

Chapter Eleven
Having The Faith

I've Made A Mistake

Who hasn't? No one is perfect in this life, so just join the club. Keep in mind though, you should not be making the same mistakes at 30 years old, that you made when you were 18! At some point, you have to grow and learn from your mistakes.

Don't ever give up hope. Know that as long as you have strength, you have the opportunity to bounce back from your mistakes.

If you have wronged someone, go to that person with a sincere heart and apologize.

Don't dwell on what you can't change. Learn to pick up the pieces and rebuild from there.

Why Me?

Troubles are not restrictive! Whether you are rich or poor, fat or thin, cute or the cutest, we are all prone to trials and tribulations.

Life is not always fair, but life is good. When troubles come your way (and they will), pick yourself up and move forward.

Run the race, fight the fight and weather the storm. Truly, troubles don't last always.

Trials really do make us stronger and wiser.

It's Not That Serious

Let go and let God! Stress will kill you. It will make you look and feel old before your time. It will break your spirit and keep you depressed and sick.

What you can change, change and leave the rest to take care of itself.

We are often guilty of blowing things out of proportion. However, when you look back at the situation, you see that it wasn't really all that bad.

Learn to eliminate stress in your life.

Thank The Lord

Every day that you rise, thank the Lord. Every time you can feed your own self, thank the Lord. For every flower you can smell, thank the Lord.

When depression comes your way, find something to thank the Lord for. Learn to turn your negatives into positives. Learn to look for the good in people and the good in life.

You will be surprised how your mind can control your feelings. Instead of feeling sad about not having that new car you wanted, thank the Lord for giving you feet to walk with. When depressed about not getting that new job, thank the Lord for having a job period.

Let your mind turn that negative into a positive...just say, thank you Lord for another day!

Psalms 106:1
Give thanks to the Lord, for He is good.

Prayer Changes Things

You will have challenges and trials in your life. There will be times when you just don't know what to do. Times when you don't see your way clear.

Honey, get on your knees and pray. Pray like you have never prayed before!

Believe me, prayer has changed many people's lives. Get some good prayer warriors in your life.

Let the Lord know what you need and what is wrong. However, before you fall on your knees asking for this, that and the other, make sure you have let go of the hate and ill feelings you are holding against others.

Don't let hate and bitterness block your blessings.

Fear Not

Fear will prevent you from living and enjoying life. It will keep you from learning and growing. There is a whole world out there for your pleasure.

Don't live life on "what ifs." Too scared to do and too scared to go, thinking what if this, that or the other happens. Learn to pray and go for it.

But babe, use common sense; don't go scuba diving by yourself when you don't even know how to swim. Please don't let me find out that you're climbing Mt. Everest by yourself, trying to show everyone that you are now discovering the new you.

Use good judgment in your decisions.

I Don't Want To Live Anymore

The hell you don't! Girl, don't even talk this way. Life is so very good. You will have problems and challenges in life, but you can make it through. There is nothing so bad in life that you can't bounce back from.

Keep in mind that you are not alone. Nine times out of ten, what you're going through, someone else has gone through. You are not the first, and you won't be the last.

There is help available.

My friend left too early. She was in the prime of her life. Looking from the outside in, she had it all. She was often told by her peers how blessed she was and how others would love to be in her shoes. We were happier for her than she was for herself.

We all are guilty of wishing our lives were different. Comparing our life to others, even those we see in the movies.

Ladies, we have to look within and know that life is worth living.

Strength gives you ability
Ability gives you a chance
A chance gives you courage
Courage gives you power
Power gives you the ability to fight and the ability to win

You've been invited to your friend's Christmas party, but you're too scared to go. You felt that you wouldn't know how to dress, or how to act.

A week ago, you were invited to a fancy restaurant, and again you didn't want to go because you doubted yourself.

Let me tell you something! Anything you don't know how to do, you can learn to do. Have no shame in your game. You can find a book on any subject. Buy yourself a book on etiquette and keep it handy. Use the Internet for help, and don't be too shy to ask someone you trust.

Stop looking at so much television, listening to the radio and talking on the telephone. Pick up a book and open your mind to a world of knowledge, power and wisdom.

The Sound Of Music...

Whether it's the guitar, flute, piano or saxophone, learn to play an instrument. You will be surprised how soothing music can relax your mind.

Playing an instrument can take you to another level of peace and happiness. Not only will this benefit your mental state, it may just open doors for you to earn extra money.

Hire yourself out to play at weddings, Barmitzvah, or at parties. Can you imagine being paid to do something you enjoy doing?

One day, you may just have your own tutoring company, or create an entertainment business with other talented young musicians (and play at different social events).

Learn to use your talents to your benefit.

Believe me; I feel for you, as well as your friends and peers, because some things have really changed.

I hear mothers' concerns about what choices their young girls will have to choose from when it's time for marriage. Even dating is hard enough these days.

Back in the day, a young man would walk, ride his bike, or catch the bus to come and see you. Back in the day that young man naturally paid for you and him to go to the movies, however, now things are so expensive, that the young man may say, "Let's go dutch."

Most guys loved their girlfriends going to church. Now they will ask, why are you going to that church? Let's go to Jerry's party instead.

And yes sex was always around, but back in the day the thought of catching a deadly sexual disease (like AIDS) wasn't even a thought. If you did catch a dreadful STD, it could simply be treated with Penicillin! Honey, things have changed.

We as mothers wonder how our daughters will ever be able to afford a home, even an apartment, because rent is so high. Look around; have you noticed that young adults are not moving away from home like they used to?

Honey, we are aware of the fact that you will have challenges; however, we had them also. Some were the same, yet some are so different.

But just as we stayed strong, focused and determined, you will have to do the same.

There are new doors of opportunity available for you. Now in our day, we never knew what the Internet was. Most of us never owned a computer.

Take advantage of knowledge and new opportunities that are available to you.

Keep the faith!

Chapter Twelve
Rewind-Fast Forward

Mother, Stop Worrying

That is like telling a baby not to cry. Some mothers may worry more than others, but every mother has concern for their child. I believe every mother's dream is to live long enough to see her child grown, independent and happy.

Kids often think that their parents are trying to control and run their lives (believe me this is not normally the case). We are just trying to guide you in the right direction, so that you can be successful in life. And keep in mind, success does not mean you have to be rich. Most mothers' idea of success is that you become a responsible adult, making an honest living.

Most kids want parents in their lives when it's convenient for them (when they need money, the car or clothes, etc.). However, when it comes down to trying to teach and direct them, that's when they feel we are all in their business.

Well kids, if you learn nothing else, learn that you can never understand a mother's love for her child. Most mothers would lay down their life for their child. What other person is so forgiving of your faults and mistakes? When everyone else has turned their backs on you, your mother is still there standing by your side. When you hurt, we hurt.

God appointed us as mothers, and with that comes responsibilities. We as mothers are only doing what a mother should do, and that is to teach and guide you.

Babes, please give us some credit for knowing more than you, if for no other reason than we have lived beyond your years. We, too, were young ladies (teenagers at one time). And believe me, we have some stories to tell.

Hopefully one day you will experience what it is to love a child, to want the best for that child, and to sacrifice for that child. One day, you will look back and say, ***"Now I understand how my mother felt!"***

Babes, we are guilty of loving you and trying to protect you. Remember the time I asked you if you could you imagine life without me? And you said, "No!" Well honey, I don't ever want to know what life would be like without you. This is why I try so hard to direct and protect you.

Baby girl, I'm learning to let go, but be patient with me, because being a mother is a learning experience. I'm not perfect; therefore, I am still trying to get it right!

There's No Place Like Home

I know you loved your blue room with the queen size bed, the television, DVD and CD player, and having your own bathroom decorated just the way you wanted it. When you surfaced from your room, you enjoyed hogging the big screen television while looking at your music videos and cable TV.

Well honey, you had it made! But remember when I used to tell you that this wasn't the real world? Now that you are on your own, don't be disappointed about not having it like it was at home. Let's face facts, you were spoiled, and you were blessed.

You may hit some road bumps, and you may have to crawl before you walk, but you can make it. Keep thinking how you hated the way I decorated and you decided that you couldn't wait to get your own place, because you were going to have it all laid out your way!

Stay excited and determined to meet your goals and your dreams. Don't live in the past, but look towards the future. Be determined to have your own.

I can hardly wait for the day when you will have us over for dinner at your place.

Believe it or not, we have been where you are, and where you're headed. You think we are naive to what's happening, but we're not!

The same things you are thinking, we thought. The same tight clothes you wear, we have worn. The parties and the boys, we've been there, too.

So baby, stop thinking we don't have a clue. Just like our parents taught us, we're attempting to teach you, and believe it or not, you will be trying to teach it to your kids one day.

Perfect example: I'm sure you can't imagine your parents having sex, but how do you think you got here (ha-ha)? Haven't you ever wondered how we know when you're lying? Because we, too, at one time have used that same lie in the past (with our parents).

We as parents are only doing what you will (should) be doing one day, trying to direct you and keep you from making some of the same mistakes we made.

Back in the day, a neighbor would spank you if you did something wrong.
Back in the day, you could find a good job with no college degree.
Back in the day, you fought with hands, and not with weapons.
Back in the day, we didn't eat fast foods several times a week.
Back in the day, you went to Sunday School/church every Sunday.
On and on and on...

Basically, what I'm saying is, time does bring about a change; however, some things never change. We as mothers know what it is to want to party, have fun and have boyfriends. We know there are temptations out there that you will have to face. We simply want you to know that we, too, had some of these same temptations. We also know the price that has to be paid when giving into some of these temptations. We know what it is to hurt, to cry, and to wonder why!

Was It Really That Bad?

Okay, you are now on your own. You are doing all the cleaning, cooking and paying of the bills. You have even learned how to pick a good melon at the grocery store.

Remember when I would tell you to turn off the light if you're not in that room? Well I see you are now doing the same. You are now forced to cut back on your expenses. You and Cup Of Noodles have become best friends (when your funds are low). I used to be the one telling you to turn down that radio; well, now it's your landlord telling you.

What about those good old days when you were at home and opened the refrigerator and could choose from apple, orange or grape juice? Well, now you are drinking an off brand, watered down orange juice.

I got your message, honey, that your car wouldn't start, the toilet overflowed and your closet door is off track; well, I hate to tell you, but your dad is not home; you will have to call a repairman.

Honey, stop crying! You are simply going through what every independent adult goes through.

But answer me this! Now looking back, was it really that bad at home?

Baby girl, it's all up to you. I have laid the foundation, I have cried, screamed and prayed. You are now responsible for you. If you succeed or fail, it's your decision. You were given direction and much love. I have always offered you guidance and support.

You are at the age of accountability, with a sound mind (hopefully, ha-ha). You and only you will be responsible for your decisions. You and only you will have to decide the path you will choose to take. You can either take the high road, or you can take the low road.

Honey, either you will buckle under pressure, or the pressure will only make you stronger. You will stand for something, or fall for anything. You will choose to stay focused or fall by the wayside. Will you believe and trust in God, or will you run to alcohol and drugs for your comfort zone?

Hopefully, something I did or said will benefit your decisions on how you choose your path. I have prayed and will continue to pray that you will make wise choices in your life; a life that you are now responsible for.

It's all up to you!

I'm Out Of Here

Yea baby girl, I hate to think about this, but I'm gone. As sure as we live, we will also die one day! My time on this earth is over, and you're scared that you won't survive without me.

Well, honey, that is hogwash. You will be just fine, because I prepared you well. That is why I did what I did by teaching you this, that and the other. Remember when I taught you how to balance a checking account, and how to pay bills? I even made you call and schedule your doctor and dentist appointments at a young age. I had the toughest time making you learn how to wash, cook and clean, but babe, you learned how to iron better than I did.

Honey, you will know how to survive. No one will be able to pull the wool over your eyes. Your counterparts will wonder how you know what you know.

Your response will be, "Oh, my mom taught me how!"

See, you will be just fine...

DOMESTIC VIOLENCE
800 799-SAFE
888 END-ABUSE

EATING DISORDERS
800 931-2237

IRS
800 829-1040

SUICIDE
800 784-2433

SEX - AIDS
800 342-AIDS

Helpful Hints

Carpet Spills - blot up spill first, and saturate carpet with club soda or Windex.

Newspaper - excellent for cleaning windows.

Need to dust fast - put an old pair of socks on each hand, and go to work.

Preventing soap scum on shower door - wax shower door after cleaning it.

Left over tea, coffee or lemonade - freeze in ice cub containers.

To soften rock hard brown sugar - put a piece of apple in the canister.

To store recipes - put them inside the plastic sheets of a photo album

To keep cookies fresh - put a piece of bread in jar

To keep bugs from cereal & flour - put a bay leaf or stick of spearmint gum on the shelf.

Ironing an item in the morning - store it in the refrigerator the night before (it makes it easier to iron the item).

Broken pieces of glass - wet a paper towel and pick up gently.

If you can't afford wrapping paper - use newspaper, and attach a pretty bow.

Extra throw blankets - put them inside pillow shams.

Baking Soda - use it to keep your refrigerator fresh.

Money Saving Ideas

Baby sit
Elderly sitting
Start a mobile car washing service
Pet sitter (walker)
House sitting service
Bake & sell cookies or brownies
Buy in bulk (split cost with a friend)
Clip coupons
Cook a large pot of beans or stew/it's filling and goes a long way
Shop at bargain discount stores
Check for sale items
Put items in layaway
Buy more washable clothes (no need to create a cleaning bill)
Check books out at the library, instead of buying them
Check movies out at the library, instead of buying or renting them
Learn to braid, perm, wash & blow dry friends hair
Learn to wax unwanted hairs for friends
Recycle
Create your own window/mini blind cleaning service
Tutor a child
Cleaning house service (even the dorms at school)
Create a shoeshine service for new recruits
Take your lunch
Type and edit term papers

Cheap Health & Beauty Secrets

Baking soda can be used as toothpaste, deodorant and a face scrub.

New pimple on the face - dab white toothpaste on the pimple at bedtime; or you can mix milk of magnesia or cornstarch with rubbing alcohol and it will create a paste, and apply it to the pimple.

Swollen pimples - hold an ice cube on the pimple. It will reduce the swelling and the redness.

Hiccups - to stop hiccups, (adults) try eating a spoonful of sugar. You can also try covering your ears with your fingers and drink through a straw.

Lavender Essential Oil is excellent for sunburn.

Lemon wedges are excellent for age spots and dark spots.

Pour a cup of powdered milk under running bath water to remove dry skin. It will leave you feeling baby soft.

Cold sore beginning, dab some Pepto Bismol on the spot before the sore has a chance to appear.

Puffy eyes - place cool slices of cucumber over the eyes and rest for a while.

Mayonnaise is a great hair conditioner.

Olive Oil is a good moisturizer for the skin and hair.

And The Saying Goes

Many are called, but few are chosen
Birds of a feather, flock together
The apple don't fall far from the tree
Wrong as two left shoes
What is done in the dark will soon come to light
A picture is worth a thousand words
Straight as an arrow
Thick as thieves
Pure as the driven snow
An ounce of prevention is worth a pound of cure
A penny saved is a penny earned
Wise as an owl
Patience is a virtue
Stubborn as a mule
Happy as a lark
To thine own self be true
It's water under the bridge
Waste not want not
You never miss your water til the well runs dry
One monkey don't stop the show
Don't cry over spilled milk
Two wrongs don't make it right
Beggars can't be choosey
It's not over till the fat lady sings
Don't put off tomorrow what you can do today
He's one short of a six-pack
You made your bed, now lie in it
Trouble don't last always
Green with envy
Believe half of what you see and none of what you hear
When Hell freezes over
Why buy the cow when you can get the milk free?
Better late, than never
You are judged by the company you keep

Mom, I Have Something To Tell You

I Can't Help But Wonder

This may be the hardest page for me to type. Tears come to my eyes at the thought of my own mother. This is a subject I ponder if I should even touch upon. In no way am I discrediting my own mom and her mothering skills, because I truly believe she did the best she could under her own circumstances.

She is no longer here to defend or explain her own actions; therefore, I can only speak on my feelings. My mom may have felt just as lonely as I have. She, too, may have wondered why!

I can't help but wonder if I would have been a better, stronger and wiser lady if I had received more emotional love. I can't help but wonder what it would have been like to hear my mom say...

I love you
I am proud of you
You are beautiful
You are intelligent
I'm here for you

I can't help but wonder what it would have felt like to hold hands with my mother. I wonder what it would have been like to feel the touch of my mother's kiss on my cheek. Oh, and I wonder how it would have been to hear my mother say, "You can talk to me about anything!" I wonder if I had cried in front of her; would she have hugged me and told me that everything will be all right.

Just maybe the lack of emotion from my mom made me more loving and open with you. Just maybe I owe her for making me be a better mom to you.

Courtney, I love you. I am proud of you. I am here for you. You are beautiful. You are smart. I support you.

156 / Brenda Hayes

One day while at church the minister said, "Close your eyes and think back to a beautiful and happy time..." I thought of you.

Love, Mom

BOOK AVAILABLE THROUGH
Milligan Books, Inc.

Moving Out And Moving On $14.95

Order Form

Milligan Books, Inc.
1425 W. Manchester Ave., Suite C, Los Angeles, CA 90047
(323) 750-3592

Name_____ Date _____

Address_____

City_____ State____ Zip Code _____

Day Telephone _____

Evening Telephone_____

Book Title_____

Number of books ordered___ Total ....$ _____

Sales Taxes (CA Add 8.25%) ....$ _____

Shipping & Handling $4.90 for one book ..$ _____

Add $1.00 for each additional book ....$ _____

Total Amount Due......................................$ _____

☐ Check ☐ Money Order ☐ Other Cards _____

☐ Visa ☐ MasterCard Expiration Date _____

Credit Card No. _____

Driver License No. _____

Make check payable to Milligan Books, Inc.

_____ _____

Signature   Date